ABT

Team Spirit

THE PHILADELPHIA 76ers

BY

MARK STEWART

Content Consultant
Matt Zeysing
Historian and Archivist
The Naismith Memorial Basketball Hall of Fame

NORWOODHOUSE PRESS

CHICAGO, ILLINOIS

Norwood House Press
P.O. Box 316598
Chicago, Illinois 60631

For information regarding Norwood House Press, please visit our website at:
www.norwoodhousepress.com or call 866-565-2900.

All photos courtesy of AP Images—AP/Wide World Photos, Inc. except the following:
Author's Collection (7, 26, 34 right, 35 top left, 36, 41 top);
David Dow/NBAE/Getty Images (cover); Jesse D. Garrabrant/NBAE/Getty Images (12);
Larry Berman/BermanSports.com (8, 22); Topps, Inc. (14, 20, 21, 30, 34 left, 40 both, 43);
Black Book Archives/John Klein (39).
Special thanks to Topps, Inc.

Editor: Mike Kennedy
Associate Editor: Brian Fitzgerald
Designer: Ron Jaffe
Project Management: Black Book Partners, LLC.
Special thanks to John Verzella.

Library of Congress Cataloging-in-Publication Data

Stewart, Mark, 1960-
  The Philadelphia 76ers / by Mark Stewart ; content consultant,
Matt Zeysing.
      p. cm. -- (Team spirit)
   Summary: "Presents the history, accomplishments and key person-
alities of the Philadelphia 76ers basketball team. Includes timelines,
quotes, maps, glossary and websites"--Provided by publisher.
   Includes bibliographical references and index.
   ISBN-13: 978-1-59953-125-0 (lib. bdg. : alk. paper)
   ISBN-10: 1-59953-125-9 (lib. bdg. : alk. paper)
   1. Philadelphia 76ers (Basketball team)--History--Juvenile litera-
ture. I. Zeysing, Matt. II. Title.
GV885.52.P5S84 2008
796.323'640974811--dc22

                                              2007010784

Manufactured in the United States of America.

COVER PHOTO: The 76ers celebrate a win at home over the Utah Jazz
during the 2006–07 season.

Table of Contents

SPORTS WORDS & VOCABULARY WORDS: In this book, you will find many words that are new to you. You may also see familiar words used in new ways. The glossary on page 46 gives the meanings of basketball words, as well as "everyday" words that have special basketball meanings. These words appear in **bold type** throughout the book. The glossary on page 47 gives the meanings of vocabulary words that are not related to basketball. They appear in ***bold italic type*** throughout the book.

BASKETBALL SEASONS: Because each basketball season begins late in one year and ends early in the next, seasons are not named after years. Instead, they are written out as two years separated by a dash, for example 1944–45 or 2005–06.

Meet the 76ers

Basketball has a long and wonderful history in Philadelphia, Pennsylvania. Some of the game's greatest players have learned their craft on the city's playgrounds and in its gyms. From high school to college to the **professional** game, Philadelphia has been one of the shining stars in the basketball universe for more than 100 years.

The Philadelphia 76ers are an important part of this *tradition*. The "Philly Game" is a special mix of attitude and style. Every player who wears the 76ers' uniform must uphold the city's basketball reputation. Win or lose, Philadelphia always plays for pride.

This book tells the story of the 76ers. They have a way of finding special, creative players who raise basketball to a form of art. But the 76ers are more than a collection of stars. The team knows how to blend the talent on its **roster** to build a winner. Each year, the 76ers write another chapter in the basketball story of Philadelphia.

Willie Green is congratulated by Kyle Korver after a win by the 76ers during the 2006–07 season.

Way Back When

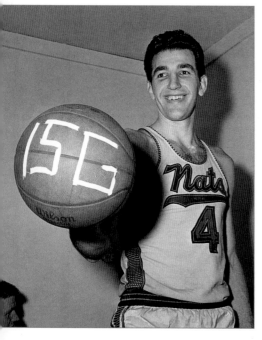

The 76ers may call Philadelphia their home, but they were "born and raised" in upstate New York. A man named Danny Biasone started the team in the city of Syracuse in the late 1930s and called it the Nationals—or "Nats," for short. They would spend more than 20 years there before moving to Pennsylvania. During that time, another club known as the Warriors played in Philadelphia.

The Nationals were part of the **National Basketball League (NBL)** until 1949. That year, the NBL joined forces with another league called the Basketball Association of America (BAA) to become the **National Basketball Association (NBA)**. The Nationals were one of the NBA's toughest teams. No club hustled more or played harder on defense.

Syracuse's top star was a quick and powerful forward named Dolph Schayes. His teammates included Paul Seymour, Red Rocha, Earl Lloyd, George King, and Al Cervi, who also coached the Nationals. They made it to the NBA Finals in 1950 and 1954 but lost both times. In 1954–55, Syracuse added a young center named Johnny Kerr, and the Nationals won the NBA Championship.

Eight years later, the Nationals moved to Philadelphia and were renamed the 76ers. The year before, in 1962, fans in Philadelphia had been disappointed when the Warriors left for San Francisco, California. They were overjoyed to welcome their new team.

The fans were even happier when the 76ers traded with San Francisco for Wilt Chamberlain in 1965. Chamberlain had grown up in Philadelphia. Playing in his hometown with the Warriors, he had

1967 Philadelphia 76ers
FRONT ROW: Wilt Chamberlain, Dave Gambee, Luke Jackson, Bill Cunningham, Chet Walker
STANDING: Al Domenico, Trainer; Alex Hannum, Coach; Wally Jones, Bill Melchionni,
Matt Guokas, Hal Greer, Larry Costello; Irv Kosloff, President; Jack Ramsay, General Manager

become the NBA's greatest scorer. His return to Philadelphia made the 76ers into a powerhouse.

In 1966–67, the 76ers set a record by winning 68 games. The team surrounded Chamberlain with several talented players, including Hal Greer, Wali Jones, Chet Walker, Luke Jackson, and Billy Cunningham. Philadelphia defeated the Warriors in the NBA Finals to win the championship.

LEFT: Dolph Schayes celebrates after scoring his 15,000th point in 1963.
ABOVE: A souvenir of the 1966–67 Philadelphia team, which won 68 games.

The 76ers continued their winning ways in the 1970s, thanks to stars such as Julius Erving, George McGinnis, Caldwell Jones, Darryl Dawkins, Doug Collins, and World B. Free. Still, Philadelphia's next title did not come until 1982–83. Cunningham, a member of the 1967 championship team, coached the 76ers. On the court, Erving teamed up with Maurice Cheeks and Moses Malone, who was voted the league's **Most Valuable Player (MVP)**. The 76ers won 65 games during the regular season and lost only once in the **playoffs** on the way to the NBA Championship.

Over the next 20 years, the 76ers had some of the league's top players, including Charles Barkley, Hersey Hawkins, Jerry Stackhouse, and Allen Iverson. In 2000–01, Iverson and Dikembe Mutombo led Philadelphia back to the NBA Finals, but the 76ers lost to the Los Angeles Lakers.

LEFT: Julius Erving soars for a slam dunk against the New Jersey Nets.
ABOVE: Allen Iverson looks for an opening as he dribbles down the court.

The Team Today

During the 2006–07 season, the 76ers made a decision to rebuild their team around a new *generation* of stars. After Philadelphia traded Allen Iverson to the Denver Nuggets, the spotlight began to shine on players such as Andre Iguodala, Kyle Korver, Samuel Dalembert, Andre Miller, and Rodney Carney.

As other young stars join the team through trades and the **NBA draft**, the 76ers will concentrate on the things that have made them successful in the past. They will attack the basket, fight for every rebound and **loose ball**, and make their opponents work hard for every point.

The 76ers have always been patient with their young players. They have also been smart when they trade for experienced stars. This *strategy* has paid off in nine trips to the NBA Finals during the team's history. No one doubts that the 76ers will soon be playing for a championship again.

The 76ers rejoice after a victory in January 2006.

Home Court

In the early days of the NBA, no one wanted to play the Nationals in Syracuse. Their home arena, the Onondaga War Memorial, held a little more than 6,000 fans, but they were so loud that opposing players sometimes felt as if everyone was sitting in the front row.

When the team moved to Philadelphia, it played most of its games in Convention Hall. In 1967, the 76ers opened a new arena called the Spectrum. It was their first modern arena. They played there for nearly 30 years.

In 1996, the team moved to a new arena built near the Spectrum. Over the next few years, a new football stadium and baseball stadium were opened in the same *sports complex*. In 2003, the 76ers' arena became known as the Wachovia Center.

BY THE NUMBERS

- *There are 21,600 seats for basketball in the 76ers' arena.*
- *The first sporting event in the arena was a hockey game between Team USA and Team Canada. Team USA won 5–3.*
- *As of 2007, the 76ers had retired seven numbers—6 (Julius Erving), 10 (Maurice Cheeks), 13 (Wilt Chamberlain), 15 (Hal Greer), 24 (Bobby Jones), 32 (Billy Cunningham), and 34 (Charles Barkley).*

Samuel Dalembert thrills fans with a dunk during a home game against the Phoenix Suns.

Dressed for Success

The name "76ers" celebrates the patriots who declared independence from England in 1776. Not surprisingly, the team's uniform and **logo** have often included the 13 stars of the **colonial flag**—which also form the shape of a basketball. The team has used red, white, and blue in its uniforms since it played in Syracuse.

The team has had many different uniform styles over the years. When they were the Nationals, their uniform tops were too narrow to fit the team's entire name. As a result, Syracuse had to shorten the name to "Nats."

After moving to Philadelphia, the 76ers tried many different designs. For more than 30 years, their home uniforms were white and their road jerseys either blue or red. In 1997, the team made black an important uniform color and also redesigned its logo. The 76ers, however, still use red, white, and blue to remind fans of their proud history.

George McGinnis is pictured in Philadelphia's road uniform on this 1976 trading card.

76 ERS

GEORGE McGINNIS ▪ FORWARD

UNIFORM BASICS

The basketball uniform is very simple. It consists of a roomy top and baggy shorts.

- The top hangs from the shoulders, with big "scoops" for the arms and neck. This style has not changed much over the years.

- Shorts, however, have changed a lot. They used to be very short, so players could move their legs freely. In the last 20 years, shorts have gotten longer and much baggier.

Basketball uniforms look the same as they did long ago ... until you look very closely. In the old days, the shorts had belts and buckles. The tops were made of a thick cotton called "jersey," which got very heavy when players sweated. Later, uniforms were made of shiny **satin**. They may have looked great, but they did not "breathe." As a result, players got very hot! Today, most uniforms are made of **synthetic** materials that soak up sweat and keep the body cool.

Kyle Korver shoots a jump shot in the 76ers' 2006–07 black uniform.

We Won!

Basketball in the early 1950s was a test of size, strength, and *stamina*. The Nationals were not as big as other NBA teams, but no one fought harder from the opening tip-off to the final buzzer. In 1953–54, Syracuse reached the NBA Finals but lost to the Minneapolis Lakers in seven games. In 1954–55, the team returned to the finals to face the Ft. Wayne Pistons.

The Nationals won the opening game with help from a little-used substitute named Dick Farley. Dolph Schayes led Syracuse to victory in Game 2. The Pistons fought back to win the next three games. With their backs against the wall, the Nationals won Game 6, 109–104. In Game 7, they erased a 17-point Ft. Wayne lead with help from Farley and another reserve, Billy Kenville. With the score tied 91–91, guard George King sank a foul shot, and then Paul Seymour made a great defensive play to give Syracuse its first NBA Championship.

The team's next title came in 1966–67, after the club had moved to Philadelphia. The 76ers' coach, Alex Hannum, convinced Wilt Chamberlain to think less about scoring and more about teamwork. When Chamberlain began sharing the ball, players such as Hal Greer and Chet Walker made bigger contributions, and the 76ers became almost impossible to defend. Philadelphia set a record with 68 victories and then defeated the Cincinnati Royals and Boston Celtics in the playoffs.

The win over Boston was quite a triumph. It was the first time since 1956 that the Celtics did not make it to the NBA Finals. It was also the first time in his career that Chamberlain had beaten Boston's Bill Russell in the playoffs. In the NBA Finals, the 76ers won an exciting battle with the San Francisco Warriors.

LEFT: Dolph Schayes drives to the basket.   **ABOVE**: Wilt Chamberlain goes up for a shot against Bill Russell of the Celtics.

The 76ers won their third title in the spring of 1983. Billy Cunningham, a player from the 1966–67 team, was now Philadelphia's coach. His **lineup** included Julius Erving, Bobby Jones, Maurice Cheeks, and Andrew Toney. The 76ers had already made it to the NBA Finals twice in the 1980s, but both times they lost to the Los Angeles Lakers. In 1982–83, however, the 76ers had Moses Malone, a great center that the team had signed as a **free agent**. Malone had been the league MVP with the Houston Rockets the year before.

The 76ers won 65 games in Malone's first season with the team. They looked so good when the playoffs started that many thought they might not lose a single game. The team's battle cry was "Four-Four-Four," meaning that they wanted to sweep all three of their series in four games—something that had never been done. Philadelphia almost did it. They beat the New York Knicks in four games, but it took them five games in the **Eastern Conference Finals** to defeat the Milwaukee Bucks.

Against the Lakers in the NBA Finals, Malone was too much for Kareem Abdul-Jabbar. He averaged 26 points and 18 rebounds a game. The 76ers won the first two games at home and finished their championship sweep with two more victories when the series moved to Los Angeles.

LEFT: Magic Johnson can only watch as Julius Erving drives to the basket.
ABOVE: Maurice Cheeks cheers and Kareem Abdul-Jabbar ducks as Moses Malone slams one against the Lakers.

Go-To Guys

To be a true star in the NBA, you need more than a great shot. You have to be a "go-to guy"—someone teammates trust to make the winning play when the seconds are ticking away in a big game. Fans of the 76ers and Nationals have had a lot to cheer about over the years, including these great stars …

THE PIONEERS

DOLPH SCHAYES   6' 8" Forward

• BORN: 5/19/1928   • PLAYED FOR TEAM: 1948–49 TO 1963–64

Dolph Schayes had a good outside shot and great inside moves. He could also run and jump like a guard and was a rugged defender. He was one of the best free-throw shooters in history, too. When Schayes retired, he held the NBA career records for points and games played.

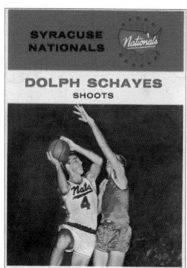

JOHNNY KERR   6' 9" Center

• BORN: 7/17/1932

• PLAYED FOR TEAM: 1954–55 TO 1964–65

Johnny Kerr was a good scorer and rebounder, but what made him stand out was his passing. When Kerr had his hands on the ball, the defense did not know who would put it in the hoop.

HAL GREER   6' 2" Guard

- BORN: 6/26/1936   • PLAYED FOR TEAM: 1958–59 TO 1972–73

There were no *flaws* in Hal Greer's game. He did everything an NBA guard needs to do and did it better—and longer—than almost anyone in history. Greer was one of the most respected leaders in the league.

WILT CHAMBERLAIN   7' 1" Center

- BORN: 8/21/1936   • DIED: 10/12/1999
- PLAYED FOR TEAM: 1964–65 TO 1967–68

With the 76ers, Wilt Chamberlain devoted his energy to playing **team basketball** and led Philadelphia to the 1966–67 championship. Chamberlain was the league's MVP in each of his three full seasons with the 76ers.

BILLY CUNNINGHAM   6' 6" Forward

- BORN: 6/3/1943   • PLAYED FOR TEAM: 1965–66 TO 1971–72 & 1974–75 TO 1975–76

No one on the 76ers played with more *intensity* or fire than Billy Cunningham. He was a great leaper whose shot was almost impossible to defend. Cunningham had more than 2,000 points and 1,000 rebounds in the same season twice for the 76ers.

BILLY CUNNINGHAM = F

LEFT: Dolph Schayes   **ABOVE**: Billy Cunningham

21

MODERN STARS

DOUG COLLINS 6' 6" Guard

• BORN: 7/28/1951   • PLAYED FOR TEAM: 1973–74 TO 1980–81

Doug Collins supplied whatever the 76ers needed in a game. He had a good outside shot, quick hands on defense, and could start or finish a **fast break** as well as any guard in the NBA.

JULIUS ERVING 6' 7" Forward

• BORN: 2/22/1950   • PLAYED FOR TEAM: 1976–77 TO 1986–87

When Julius Erving had a basketball in his hands, it was like watching an artist with a paintbrush. He combined tremendous skill with great creativity to bring fans out of their seats with his twisting drives and soaring dunks. Erving was nicknamed "Dr. J" for the way he "operated" on opponents.

MAURICE CHEEKS 6' 1" Guard

• BORN: 9/8/1956

• PLAYED FOR TEAM: 1978–79 TO 1988–89

Maurice Cheeks was one of the smartest and quickest players in the NBA. He was a superb passer and dribbler—and always a threat to score. Cheeks was also named to the league's **All-Defensive Team** five years in a row.

ABOVE: Julius Erving
TOP RIGHT: Charles Barkley **BOTTOM RIGHT**: Allen Iverson

MOSES MALONE   6' 10" Center

- BORN: 3/23/1955
- PLAYED FOR TEAM: 1982–83 TO 1985–86 & 1993–94

Moses Malone was extraordinary at turning missed shots into easy baskets. Frustrated opponents often fouled Malone, and he made them pay. Malone scored more than 9,000 points on free throws during his career.

CHARLES BARKLEY   6' 5" Forward

- BORN: 2/20/1963
- PLAYED FOR TEAM: 1984–85 TO 1991–92

Charles Barkley was one of the NBA's greatest **power forwards**—even though he was shorter than many guards! Barkley combined a wide body with great *agility* and timing to earn the nickname the "Round Mound of Rebound." He was famous for his huge appetite—and for making *outrageous* and funny comments.

ALLEN IVERSON   6' 0" Guard

- BORN: 6/7/1975
- PLAYED FOR TEAM: 1996–97 TO 2006–07

Allen Iverson was amazingly quick. His lightning-fast **crossover dribble** left the league's best defenders in the dust. Iverson's fearless, attacking style led the 76ers to the NBA Finals in 2001.

On the Sidelines

The 76ers have had some great coaches over the years. Going back to their days as the Syracuse Nationals, the team has often hired former players to work on the sidelines. Al Cervi, who led the team to the NBA Championship in 1955, was a **player-coach** for many years with Syracuse.

Other players who "graduated" to coach the team include Paul Seymour, Dolph Schayes, Billy Cunningham, Matt Guokas, and Fred Carter. Maurice Cheeks, Philadelphia's great guard during the 1980s, was hired to coach the 76ers in 2005.

Although the 76ers fell short of winning the NBA Championship in 2000–01, their coach that season will always be remembered for doing a great job. Larry Brown surrounded Philadelphia's star, Allen Iverson, with a group of hardworking players. He convinced the 76ers that the key to winning was playing great defense. Brown and Iverson argued all the time about strategy. However, they shared the same goal, and in the end, they worked together to lead Philadelphia to the NBA Finals.

76ers coach Maurice Cheeks talk things over with Andre Iguodala on the sidelines.

One Great Day

During the 1960s, basketball fans loved to argue about who was the NBA's greatest guard. Some said it was Oscar Robertson. Others claimed it was Jerry West. Because of these two superstars, Hal Greer of the 76ers never got the attention he deserved. At the 1968 NBA **All-Star Game**, Greer showed just how good he was.

With the largest crowd in All-Star history packed into New York's Madison Square Garden, the East built a 64–59 lead in the first half. Greer did not do much to help his teammates. He played little in the first two quarters and scored only two points.

In the second half, the West battled back to go ahead 75–73 with seven minutes left in the third quarter. Alex Hannum—coach of the East squad and the 76ers—looked down the bench at Greer and told him to go into the game. At that point, Philadelphia center Wilt Chamberlain and Greer decided to play the **two-man game** they had perfected as teammates on the 76ers.

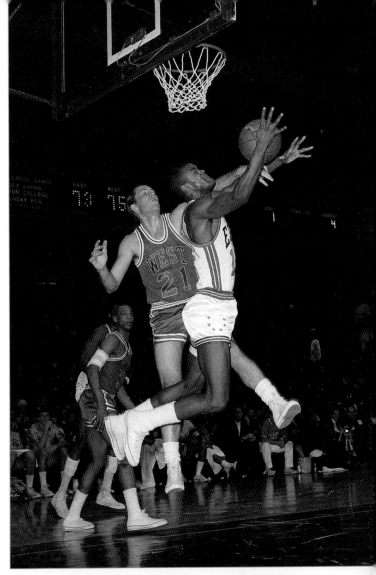

Chamberlain would take a pass at center, wait for Greer to lose his man, and then whip him a pass for an open shot. In three magical minutes, Greer scored 14 points. This started a 22–6 run that helped the East win the game 144–124. Greer ended up scoring 19 points in the third quarter alone.

Though Greer played only 17 of 48 minutes, he finished with a total of 21 points. He made each of the eight shots he took from the floor and added five foul shots in seven attempts. When the final buzzer sounded, Greer was named the All-Star Game MVP. The 19 points he scored in the third period set a record that lasted for 29 years—and reminded basketball fans everywhere what a special player Greer was.

LEFT: Hal Greer
ABOVE: Greer fights for a rebound during the 1968 All-Star Game.

Legend Has It

Did the 24-second shot clock "save" the NBA?

LEGEND HAS IT that it did. In the early 1950s, fans complained that NBA games were slow and boring. Teams could hold the ball as long as they wanted and often stalled for extended stretches at the end of games. With ticket sales falling and teams losing money, the NBA was in deep trouble. Danny Biasone, the owner of the Nationals, suggested that the league make teams shoot the ball at least once every 24 seconds. The NBA took Biasone's advice. The 24-second clock was used in 1954–55, and its *impact* was clear. Games were more exciting, and the league began to win back the fans it had lost and attract new fans, too.

Danny Biasone stands in front of his most famous creation.

What was Wilt Chamberlain's favorite nickname?

LEGEND HAS IT that he liked being called the "Big Dipper." He got the nickname in high school, because he had to dip his head when he entered a classroom. Chamberlain was also called "Goliath" and "Wilt the Stilt." He disliked both of these nicknames.

Who made the greatest shot in the history of the NBA Finals?

LEGEND HAS IT that Julius Erving did. In Game 4 of the 1980 NBA Finals against the Los Angeles Lakers, Erving had the ball near the **baseline**. He drove past Mark Landsberger and began to rise toward the hoop. Coming to meet him was Kareem Abdul-Jabbar. Erving hung in the air, floated past the 7' 2" center, and reached around the opposite side of the hoop before flicking up a shot with his fingertips. The ball rolled into the basket for an incredible reverse layup. "I thought, 'What should we do?'" said Lakers star Magic Johnson years later. "'Should we take the ball out or should we ask him to do it again?'"

It Really Happened

When the 76ers drafted 18-year-old Darryl Dawkins in 1975, they knew he would become one of the strongest players in the NBA. They just did not realize how strong. Dawkins loved to dunk, and he often joked that one day he would shatter a backboard. During a game against the Kings in Kansas City in 1979, Dawkins actually did.

Early in the second half of the game, the 6' 11" center received a pass near the basket. He soared to the rim past Bill Robinzine of the Kings and slammed the ball through with both hands. The glass backboard exploded, raining jagged **shards** on Dawkins, Robinzine, and everyone else standing nearby. For a second or two after it happened, no one moved. The entire arena was silent. Then the players started laughing, and the crowd erupted in cheers.

A clean-up crew spent an hour picking up all of the glass. Dawkins collected a few pieces for souvenirs. The Kings threatened to hand him a bill for the damage.

Robinzine had a small cut bandaged, but the wound to his pride was more serious. After the game, he learned that Dawkins—whose imagination matched his huge frame—had named his dunk. He called it the "Chocolate-Thunder-Flyin, Robinzine-Cryin, Teeth-Shakin, Glass-Breakin, Rump-Roastin, Bun-Toastin, Wham-Bam-I-Am Jam."

Three weeks later, Dawkins did it again. This time he blew out the backboard in a home game against the San Antonio Spurs. While the Philadelphia fans loved it, the NBA had seen enough. The league ordered that all teams install **collapsible rims**. They are still in use today.

LEFT: The size and strength of Darryl Dawkins can be seen on this trading card. **ABOVE**: Julius Erving and Kansas City's Scott Wedman watch as Dawkins and Bill Robinzine are showered by glass.

Team Spirit

Philadelphia sports fans are known for being tough on opponents and even tougher on their own players. Fans of the 76ers are no exception. They demand a full effort, win or lose. When the team plays hard, they cheer hard. If the 76ers let up, however, the fans are not bashful about letting them know how they feel.

Halftime at 76ers games is a lot of fun. The team's mascot, a giant rabbit named Hip-Hop Hare, leads a group of basketball acrobats called the Hare Raisers. The 76ers also have a dance team that performs between quarters and during timeouts.

The Philadelphia area has been crazy for basketball for many decades. The 76ers are known for reaching out into the community and bringing their team spirit directly to the fans. Each summer, World B. Free—a popular player from the 1970s—holds clinics for thousands of young players. This is one of many ways the 76ers and their fans add to Philadelphia's great basketball tradition.

Hip-Hop Hare gets the crowd pumped up with a slam dunk.

Timeline

The basketball season is played from October through June. That means each season takes place at the end of one year and halfway through the next. In this timeline, the accomplishments of the 76ers and Nationals are shown by season.

1946–47
The team joins the National Basketball League as the Syracuse Nationals.

1963–64
The team moves to Philadelphia and becomes the 76ers.

1950–51
Dolph Schayes leads the NBA in rebounding.

1954–55
The Nationals win their first NBA Championship.

1966–67
The 76ers win the second championship in team history.

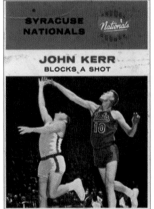

Johnny Kerr, a member of the 1955 championship team.

A button from the early days of the 76ers.

A button from the 1980s featuring Julius Erving.

Charles Barkley pulls down a rebound.

1980–81
Julius Erving is named the league's MVP.

1986–87
Charles Barkley leads the NBA in rebounding.

2000–01
The 76ers reach the NBA Finals for the ninth time.

1982–83
The 76ers win the third championship in team history.

1996–97
Allen Iverson is named NBA **Rookie of the Year**.

2004–05
Iverson wins his fourth scoring title.

Allen Iverson rises to the rim.

Fun Facts

GOOD NEWS, BAD NEWS

Five years after setting an NBA record for the most wins in a season, the 76ers set a record for the most losses. The 1966–67 team went 68–13, while the 1972–73 club won just nine games and lost 73.

A MATTER OF STYLE

Wilt Chamberlain tried everything when shooting free throws, including underhand shots. He should have asked teammate Hal Greer for a lesson. Greer took jump shots from the foul line and hit on 80 percent during his career.

HONORING A FRIEND

In 1991–92, the 76ers "unretired" Billy Cunningham's number 32 so that Charles Barkley could wear it. Barkley switched from 34 to 32 to honor his friend Magic Johnson. Johnson left the NBA that season after he tested positive for the **_AIDS virus_**.

Billy Cunningham, wearing #32 for the 76ers.

LOUD AND CLEAR

For four decades starting in 1946, Dave Zinkoff worked as the public address announcer for the Warriors and then the 76ers. Fans loved the way he yelled out the starting lineup before each home game. After Zinkoff passed away in 1985, the 76ers "retired" his microphone. The city of Philadelphia also named a street in his honor.

IN ORBIT

Dolph Schayes was a master of the two-handed **set shot**. He often made baskets from 30 feet away. Schayes's shot went so high that teammates called it "Sputnik" after the Russian satellite that was launched in the 1950s.

MASTER THIEF

In 2002–03, Allen Iverson became the first player to lead the NBA in steals three years in a row.

THE DOCTOR IS OUT

During Julius Erving's last season in the NBA, almost every player in the league autographed four giant aspirin tablets. They were presented to "Dr. J" during a ceremony to honor the defensive headaches he had caused over the years.

Talking Hoops

"Kids are great. That's one of the best things about our business, all the kids you get to meet."

—*Charles Barkley, on the energy he gets from young basketball fans*

"Right up until the time I retired at age 37, I felt like there were still things that I could do better."

—*Julius Erving, on never being satisfied as a player*

"If you're struggling with your shooting, then do other things on the basketball court. Get steals, get **assists**, get rebounds—do anything on the court to help the team win."

—*Allen Iverson, on being a complete player*

ABOVE: Charles Barkley   **RIGHT**: Wilt Chamberlain

"You try to treat everybody on the team the same. It didn't matter if it was the star or the guy who was the 12th man on the bench."

—Billy Cunningham, on the key to being a good coach

"I work hard at winning. It's as simple as that."

—Wilt Chamberlain, on the secret to being a champion

"Basketball is a game of movement and **finesse**. I built my style on running, passing, dribbling, and improving my shots."

—Dolph Schayes, on what made him the NBA's top forward in the 1950s

"I must be quick—always, always quick. The day I slow down I'm finished."

—Hal Greer, who stayed quick for 15 NBA seasons

For the Record

The great 76ers teams and players have left their marks on the record books. These are the "best of the best" …

76ERS AWARD WINNERS

WINNER	AWARD	SEASON
Wilt Chamberlain	NBA Most Valuable Player	1965–66
Dolph Schayes	NBA Coach of the Year	1965–66
Wilt Chamberlain	NBA Most Valuable Player	1966–67
Hal Greer	NBA All-Star Game MVP	1967–68
Wilt Chamberlain	NBA Most Valuable Player	1967–68
Julius Erving	NBA All-Star Game MVP	1976–77
Julius Erving	NBA Most Valuable Player	1980–81
Julius Erving	NBA All-Star Game MVP	1982–83
Bobby Jones	NBA Sixth Man Award	1982–83
Moses Malone	NBA Most Valuable Player	1982–83
Moses Malone	NBA Finals MVP	1982–83
Charles Barkley	NBA All-Star Game MVP	1990–91
Dana Barros	NBA Most Improved Player	1994–95
Allen Iverson	NBA Rookie of the Year	1996–97
Larry Brown	NBA Coach of the Year	2000–01
Aaron McKie	NBA Sixth Man Award	2000–01
Dikembe Mutombo	NBA Defensive Player of the Year	2000–01
Allen Iverson	NBA All-Star Game MVP	2000–01
Allen Iverson	NBA Most Valuable Player	2000–01
Allen Iverson	NBA All-Star Game MVP	2004–05

Julius Erving

Allen Iverson

76ERS ACHIEVEMENTS

ACHIEVEMENT	SEASON
Eastern Division Champions	1949–50*
Eastern Division Champions	1951–52*
Eastern Division Champions	1954–55*
NBA Champions	1954–55*
Eastern Division Champions	1965–66
Eastern Division Champions	1966–67
NBA Champions	1966–67
Eastern Division Champions	1967–68
Atlantic Division Champions	1976–77
Eastern Conference Champions	1976–77
Atlantic Division Champions	1977–78
Eastern Conference Champions	1979–80
Atlantic Division Champions	1980–81
Eastern Conference Champions	1981–82
Atlantic Division Champions	1982–83
Eastern Conference Champions	1982–83
NBA Champions	1982–83
Atlantic Division Champions	1989–90
Atlantic Division Champions	2000–01
Eastern Conference Champions	2000–01

Played as Syracuse Nationals

TOP: Luke Jackson, a member of the 1967 champions.
ABOVE: Charles Barkley, leader of the 1989–90 team.
LEFT: Wilt Chamberlain dunks during the 1968 All-Star Game.

41

Pinpoints

The history of a basketball team is made up of many smaller stories. These stories take place all over the map—not just in the city a team calls "home." Match the pushpins on these maps to the Team Facts and you will begin to see the story of the 76ers unfold!

TEAM FACTS

1 Syracuse, New York—*The team played here as the Nationals until 1963–64.*

2 Philadelphia, Pennsylvania—*The 76ers have played here since 1963–64.*

3 New York, New York—*Dolph Schayes was born here.*

4 Hampton, Virginia—*Allen Iverson was born here.*

5 Huntington, West Virginia—*Hal Greer was born here.*

6 Charlotte, North Carolina—*Bobby Jones was born here.*

7 Leeds, Alabama—*Charles Barkley was born here.*

8 Los Angeles, California—*Alex Hannum was born here.*

9 Chicago, Illinois—*Maurice Cheeks was born here.*

10 Port-au-Prince, Haiti—*Samuel Dalembert was born here.*

11 Miglianico, Italy—*Danny Biasone was born here.*

12 Kinshasa, Democratic Republic of Congo—*Dikembe Mutombo was born here.*

Maurice Cheeks

Play Ball

Basketball is a sport played by two teams of five players. NBA games have four 12-minute quarters—48 minutes in all—and the team that scores the most points when time has run out is the winner. Most baskets count for two points. Players who make shots from beyond the 3-point line receive an extra point. Baskets made from the free-throw line count for one point. Free throws are penalty shots awarded to a team, usually after an opponent has committed a foul. A foul is called when one player makes hard contact with another.

Players can move around all they want, but the player with the ball cannot. He must bounce the ball with one hand or the other (but never both) in order to go from one part of the court to another. As long as he keeps "dribbling," he can keep moving.

In the NBA, teams must attempt a shot within 24 seconds, so there is little time to waste. The job of the defense is to make it as difficult as possible for the offense to take a good shot—and to grab the ball if the other team shoots and misses.

This may sound simple, but anyone who has played the game knows that basketball can be very complicated. Every player on the court has a job to do. Different players have different strengths and weaknesses. The coach must mix these players in just the right way and teach them to work together as one.

The more you play and watch basketball, the more "little things" you are likely to notice. The next time you watch a game, look for these plays:

PLAY LIST

ALLEY-OOP—A play in which the passer throws the ball just to the side of the rim—so a teammate can catch it and dunk in one motion.

BACK-DOOR PLAY—A play in which the passer waits for a teammate to fake the defender away from the basket—then throws him the ball when he cuts back toward the basket.

KICK-OUT—A play in which the ball handler waits for the defense to surround him—then quickly passes to a teammate who is open for an outside shot. The ball is not really kicked in this play; the term comes from the action of pinball machines.

NO-LOOK PASS—A play in which a passer fools the defense by looking in one direction, then making a surprise pass to a teammate in another direction.

PICK-AND-ROLL—A play in which one player blocks, or "picks off," a teammate's defender with his body, then in the confusion cuts to the basket for a pass.

Glossary

BASKETBALL WORDS TO KNOW

ALL-DEFENSIVE TEAM—An honor given at the end of each season to the NBA's best defensive players at each position.

ALL-STAR GAME—The annual game in which the best players from the East and the West play against each other. The game does not count in the standings.

ASSISTS—Passes that lead to successful shots.

BASELINE—The line that runs behind the basket, from one corner of the court to the other.

COLLAPSIBLE RIMS—Special hoops that give way when great force is placed upon them.

CROSSOVER DRIBBLE—Bouncing the ball quickly from one hand to the other, enabling a dribbler to suddenly change direction.

EASTERN CONFERENCE FINALS—The playoff series that determines which team from the East will play the best team from the West for the NBA Championship.

FAST BREAK—An offensive play in which the team with the ball rushes down the court to take a shot.

FREE AGENT—A player who is allowed to sign with any team that wants him.

LINEUP—The list of players who are playing in a game.

LOOSE BALL—A ball that is not controlled by either team.

MOST VALUABLE PLAYER (MVP)—The award given each year to the league's best player; also given to the best player in the league finals and All-Star Game.

NATIONAL BASKETBALL ASSOCIATION (NBA)—The professional league that has been operating since 1946–47.

NATIONAL BASKETBALL LEAGUE (NBL)—An early professional league that played 12 seasons, from 1937–38 to 1948–49, then merged with the Basketball Association of America to become the NBA.

NBA DRAFT—The annual meeting where teams pick from a group of the best college players.

NBA FINALS—The playoff series that decides the champion of the league.

PLAYER-COACH—A person who plays for a team and coaches it at the same time.

PLAYOFFS—The games played after the season to determine the league champion.

POWER FORWARDS—The bigger and stronger of a team's two forwards.

PROFESSIONAL—A player or team that plays a sport for money. College players are not paid, so they are considered "amateurs."

ROOKIE OF THE YEAR—The annual award given to the league's best first-year player.

ROSTER—The list of players on a team.

SET SHOT—A style of shot in which a player's feet are set side-by-side on the floor, as opposed to a jump shot.

TEAM BASKETBALL—A style of play that involves everyone on the court instead of just one or two stars.

TWO-MAN GAME—A set of special plays practiced by two teammates.

OTHER WORDS TO KNOW

AGILITY—Being quick and graceful.

AIDS VIRUS—A condition that weakens the body's immune system.

COLONIAL FLAG—The flag used by the American colonists in the 1700s.

FINESSE—An artful, skilled, or delicate way of doing something.

FLAWS—Weaknesses or imperfections.

GENERATION—Period of years roughly equal to the time it takes for a person to be born, grow up, and have children.

IMPACT—A strong and immediate effect.

INTENSITY—The strength and energy of a thought or action.

LOGO—A symbol or design that represents a company or team.

OUTRAGEOUS—Wildly exaggerated.

SATIN—A smooth, shiny fabric.

SHARDS—Pieces of broken glass.

SPORTS COMPLEX—A group of structures and fields used by athletes.

STAMINA—The ability to sustain a long physical effort.

STRATEGY—A plan or method for succeeding.

SYNTHETIC—Made in a laboratory, not in nature.

TRADITION—A belief or custom that is handed down from generation to generation.

Places to Go

ON THE ROAD

PHILADELPHIA 76ERS
3601 South Broad Street
Philadelphia, Pennsylvania 19148
(215) 339-7600

NAISMITH MEMORIAL BASKETBALL HALL OF FAME
1000 West Columbus Avenue
Springfield, Massachusetts 01105
(877) 4HOOPLA

ON THE WEB

THE NATIONAL BASKETBALL ASSOCIATION   www.nba.com
  • *Learn more about the league's teams, players, and history*

THE PHILADELPHIA 76ERS   www.sixers.com
  • *Learn more about the Philadelphia 76ers*

THE BASKETBALL HALL OF FAME   www.hoophall.com
  • *Learn more about history's greatest players*

ON THE BOOKSHELF

To learn more about the sport of basketball, look for these books at your library or bookstore:

  • Thomas, Keltie. *How Basketball Works.* Berkeley, CA: Maple Tree Press, distributed through Publishers Group West, 2005.

  • Hareas, John. *Basketball.* New York, NY: Dorling Kindersley, 2005.

  • Hughes, Morgan. *Basketball.* Vero Beach, FL: Rourke Publishing, 2005.

Index

PAGE NUMBERS IN **BOLD** REFER TO ILLUSTRATIONS.

The Team

MARK STEWART has written more than 20 books on basketball, and over 100 sports books for kids. He grew up in New York City during the 1960s rooting for the Knicks and Nets, and now takes his two daughters, Mariah and Rachel, to watch them play. Mark comes from a family of writers. His grandfather was Sunday Editor of *The New York Times* and his mother was Articles Editor of *The Ladies' Home Journal* and *McCall's*. Mark has profiled hundreds of athletes over the last 20 years. He has also written several books about his native New York, and New Jersey, his home today. Mark is a graduate of Duke University, with a degree in History. He lives with his daughters and wife Sarah overlooking Sandy Hook, New Jersey.

MATT ZEYSING is the resident historian at the Basketball Hall of Fame in Springfield, Massachusetts. His research interests include the origins of the game of basketball, the development of professional basketball in the first half of the 20th century, and the culture and meaning of basketball in American society.